Katie and the Starry Night

James Mayhew

ORCHARD

For
Rebecca, Paco & Marco
and for Marlene
With love,
J. M.

With sincere thanks to everyone at Orchard Books,
especially my editor, Liz, and my designer, Clare.
Thanks also to Gabriel and the Brown family
for helping with the endpapers.

ORCHARD BOOKS
338 Euston Road, London NW1 3BH
Orchard Books Australia
Level 17/207 Kent Street, Sydney, NSW 2000
First published in 2012 by Orchard Books
First paperback publication in 2013
ISBN 978 1 40830 466 2
Text and illustrations © James Mayhew 2012
The right of James Mayhew to be identified as the author and illustrator of this book has been
asserted by him in accordance with the Copyrights, Designs and Patents Act, 1988.
A CIP catalogue record for this book is available from the British Library.
1 3 5 7 9 10 8 6 4 2
Printed in China
Orchard Books is a division of Hachette Children's Books,
an Hachette UK company.
www.hachette.co.uk

Katie and Grandma loved to go on trips together.
Sometimes, for a treat, Grandma took Katie to the art gallery.

One day, they went to see some paintings by Vincent van Gogh. Katie's favourite was called *The Starry Night*.

"It looks magical," she said. "Like a dream."

"Talking of dreams," said Grandma, "I could do with a nap."

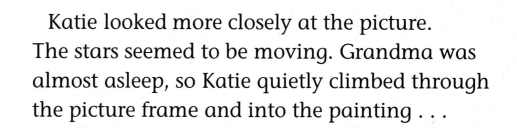

Katie looked more closely at the picture.
The stars seemed to be moving. Grandma was
almost asleep, so Katie quietly climbed through
the picture frame and into the painting . . .

The dazzling stars sparkled and swirled.
They looked close enough to touch,
so Katie reached out . . . and grasped one!
"I must show Grandma," she said,
putting the star safely in her pocket.

Jumping back into the gallery, Katie saw some other stars twirling after her.

"Perhaps they want to play!" she laughed, jumping up to catch them. But she couldn't quite reach.

"Hmm, I need something to stand on," said Katie.
She saw a picture called *Vincent's Chair*. "That's perfect!" she smiled.

Katie quickly dragged the chair out of the picture,
as more and more stars tumbled into the gallery.

But, even standing on the chair, Katie couldn't reach all the stars, and some floated into another picture called *Noon*. She decided to chase after them and so climbed through the frame.

A young couple were napping in the shade on a hot summer's day. The stars tumbled into the sky, and night soon fell upon the countryside.

The woman, whose name was Marie, woke up.

"Oh, look at all the stars!" she said. "Surely they don't belong in this painting."

"Er . . . no," said Katie, "would you help me catch them?"

Climbing up the haystack, Katie and Marie had a wonderful time jumping to catch the stars and landing in the soft hay.

But when they jumped back into the gallery, the spinning stars slipped through their fingers once again.

"We must get them back in their painting before the gallery guard sees they're missing!" said Marie.

But even Marie wasn't tall enough
to catch them.

"Look, there's a ladder!" said Katie,
spotting a picture called *The Olive Grove*.
She quickly clambered through the frame.

Women were gathering olives from a tree.

"Please, can I borrow your ladder?" asked Katie. "I have to catch some stars!"

The ladies laughed. "Ma chérie, you cannot catch stars."

"You can, with a ladder," said Katie. "Come and help me!"

They all raced back into the gallery, and the olive pickers held the ladder steady as Katie climbed up to catch the twirling stars. It was tricky work because the stars wouldn't keep still! The more Katie tried to catch them, the more they spun away.

The stars were drifting towards another painting called *Fishing Boats on the Beach*. "Come on! We must catch them!" said Marie. They all climbed inside.

In the picture, the stars were caught on a breeze and twirled out to sea.

"How will we reach them now?" asked Marie.

"Let's take a boat," said Katie.
"Oh, yes! A boat ride!" said the olive pickers, giggling.

They sailed across the sea as the stars sparkled in the sky.
"Oh, what shall we do?" worried Marie. "The stars are so high."
Katie saw a big fishing net in the boat. "Let's try this!" she said.

They all threw the net as high as they could . . . and caught the stars!
"At last!" said Katie, as everyone cheered.

Back in the gallery, they all quickly ran to *The Starry Night* picture.

"Now, we can put the stars back before the guard finds out," said Katie.

They threw the stars into the sky but it didn't look quite right.

"What's that in your pocket, Katie?" asked Marie.

"My star!" said Katie. "I wanted to show it to Grandma . . . "

"But it might float away again," said Marie. "Put it in *The Starry Night* and then you can see it whenever you want."

So, Katie threw the star up into the painting.

"Thank you, everyone," said Katie.
"We did it!"

"And now we must return to our pictures, too,"
said Marie. "Au revoir, ma chérie."
"Goodbye!" called Katie.

Katie put the chair back where it belonged, just in time, as the gallery guard came past.

"Phew!" said Katie. "Hello."

"Good afternoon," he said.

And then Grandma woke up. "Oh, I must have nodded off," she said. "I had a lovely dream about stars."

Katie giggled.

That night, Katie and Grandma looked out of the window.
It was a beautiful starry night.

"The stars look almost alive," said Grandma.

"Perhaps they are," laughed Katie.

Grandma smiled. "Perhaps," she said. "Goodnight, Katie."

VAN GOGH (1853-1890)

Born in Holland in 1853, Vincent van Gogh only began painting when he was in his twenties. Many of his most famous paintings were produced after he moved to France, where he was inspired by the vibrant colours he saw in the hot sunshine. Van Gogh experimented with his art and, although he painted what he saw, he also painted what he remembered and imagined. Yet he was often unhappy, thinking himself a failure as he only sold one picture in his lifetime. Van Gogh was frequently unwell and spent long months in hospital. Sometimes he got frustrated and, it is reported, he once became so angry it resulted in him cutting off part of his ear. Van Gogh died, unaware of how famous he would eventually become. Now he is remembered as a brave and unusual artist, one who allowed his feelings to clearly affect his unique and dazzling pictures.

The Starry Night
This is a dream-like fantasy of stars swirling above the French countryside. The contrasting blues and yellows were his favourite colours, while the wild brush strokes give a feeling of movement.

Vincent's Chair
This chair features in several pictures by Van Gogh. In this painting, it appears to be in a kitchen, as there is a box of onions nearby. Van Gogh delighted in simple rustic scenes, and rarely painted grand houses or cities.

Noon
This picture was inspired by an older painting by the artist Millet, but Van Gogh transforms the scene with the strong and exciting colours which suggest the fierce heat of a summer's day. Once again, blues and yellows dominate the picture. Van Gogh often painted ripening wheatfields in the sunshine.

The Olive Grove
The olive grove was another subject that Van Gogh painted many times in different ways, experimenting with colours. The subtler palette of this painting suggests early morning. Olive pickers often gathered crops at sunrise, before the day grew too hot to work.

Fishing Boats on the Beach
Van Gogh's bold and colourful boats are again part of an everyday scene, this time with fishermen in the distance, out at sea. The painting has a lovely and unexpected tranquillity to it.

Vincent van Gogh produced many paintings. Perhaps you are lucky enough to have one in a gallery near you. Why not try to paint some swirling skies and stars like he did? Choose colours you feel like using, and see if you can be as colourful as Van Gogh!